Horse Racing: the Statistical Route 2

A Study of the First 4 in the Betting Forecast

The First 6 Races of the Day

10 Different Types of Bet

Statistics Taken From a 1 Year Period

A simple idea, something that is easy to follow and translate into a quick and easy daily bet. Nothing difficult to understand, the first 4 horses in the betting forecast, the first 6 races on any racing day, 10 different types of bets. I applied these 10 different types of bets to those races according to the betting forecast of the Racing Post almost every day for a whole year. The work was done on a computer (excel) and I was after something that could be profitable but, easy to do; simplicity was my watchword. Not lots of ifs and buts, only do this horse if it has this or that, lots of complicated tables, money to pay to tipsters, join this or that service, spend hours having to go through lots of form etc. Just something simple and easy to follow. The trick was to find which type of bet was the most profitable in the long term and which horses in the betting forecast provided the most profit win or each way. I was not expecting a great revelation but, just something that could point me towards a possible profit and would not take up lots of my time. This book shows the end results of that period. I cannot guarantee that the same results will reoccur and only some lines proved profitable so, please be mindful of that, but it does show the type of bets and horses in the forecast that were profitable for the period July 28th 2011 to July 27th 2012 and I believe could be of interest to those that follow horses.

<u>Compiled by Mark Gaster</u>

FIRST PUBLISHED 2012

©COPYRIGHT MARK GASTER

Horse racing: the Statistical Route 2

ABOUT THE BOOK

Firstly, if reading the following appear a bit complicated; bear in mind that I am having to cover all bases and have to explain everything. In practice it is quite a simple set of data and statistics that are not hard to follow.

The first 6 races of the day were the only ones analysed along with the first 4 in the betting forecast for each of those races. The Racing Post was used as this is usually displayed in every bookmaker in the United Kingdom. It's probably the most reliable betting forecast available in the UK. The eventual starting prices could be different but, I decided to stick with the Racing Post forecast for simplicity, easiness of recording and understanding. Analysing the actual starting prices would have been a lot more difficult and harder to follow if trying to collate the actual starting prices. The betting forecast given by the UK's Daily Mirror is probably the nearest equivalent to the Racing Post but, other news papers can be entirely different and way off the mark. Outside the U.K.; an equivalent racing newspaper can be used as a substitute. But, the Racing Post was the source used to collate these statistics.

    I only assessed the first 6 races on any given day through the year for three reasons; it is simple to do, easy to relate to and does not require going through lots of races. I stuck to the first four in the betting forecasts again for simplicity and the fact that the majority of winners usually come from this area.

    I applied 10 different types of bets to all these races; they include:-
Singles, doubles, trebles, four folds, patent (first 3), lucky 15 (first 4), singles and doubles, doubles and trebles, lucky 63 and the alpha bet. I will explain these bets a bit further on for those that are not familiar with them but, these are usually the commonest types of bets used. In each case I took statistics for both Win and Each Way (E/W).

    The book comes in two parts; the first part looks at individual types of races i.e. handicap, non handicaps, hurdles, chases, flat and all weather. These were further divided into number of runners i.e. 0-7 runners, 8-11 runners, 12-15 runners and 16+ runners. I will explain this in more detail at the beginning of Part 1 but, this first part is not the most important aspect of the book but, I felt it may interest some readers and worth including.

    The second part is easier and less complicated and only looks at the statistics for all the races together without any division into type or runners and is more focused on the bets. This second part contains the details of the main thrust of this book and will probably be of more interest to the reader.

Horse Racing: the Statistical Route 2

ABOUT STATISTICS

A lot of people mistrust statistics and I can understand why. Lots of people have an axe to grind or a point to prove and will often use statistics to put them across. But, the temptation to massage them or leave out any statistics that show a different result is too great sometimes. But, they get found out eventually and statistics get a bad name and it does not matter that it is the person that has been dishonest. I have no axe to grind and I am not trying to convince you of some complicated theory; just giving you the facts as I found them. I will leave you to make your own judgement if they are useful or not but, please do not base your judgement on any suspicion that they are dishonest in any way. I have no reason or desire to convince you of anything and am quite happy just to let the statistics speak for themselves.

I would also like to say that **all the profit/loss margins in this book are either to £1 level stake (50p E/W) or to a daily bet of £3 whichever is appropriate.** I state this because how often do you see £7000 profit made last month by the tipster Joe Bloggs! What they don't tell you are that may have been the first profit made in quite a while; nothing illegal, nothing dishonest; just plain misleading. Further, they probably have that down to £200 level stakes these days. How many people can afford to bet on every tip given by a tipster at that rate especially if they are tipping every race? Even if it was one race a day that's £6,000 a month; £120,000 a month approx if they tip every race and imagine you just happened to pick a bad month to start following a particular tipster. So, I have kept it simple and a low stake level; it is easy to calculate if you wish to increase the margins for yourself. I am not a tipster; I have no special information or insight and will just show the results and leave it for you to judge without any misleading on my part.

Also, I am not going to advise where and how to invest your money; that's a decision for you to make also. I do give my own opinion in places and say what I think or what I may do but, they are only my opinions. But, please do not let that distract you from making your own assessments and judgements.

Horse Racing: the Statistical Route 2
HOW THE INFORMATION WAS COLLECTED

Nothing to complicated about this; I simply used a betting slip each day and looked for the first race on the racing card according to the Racing Post which is usually supplied in each book makers. I would note the time, the type of race, hh, nch etc and then the amount of runners in the race. I then wrote down the names of each horse according to the forecast for each race as per the Racing Post. Later I would note down where each of these four horses had come in their respective races and the odds. Day by day I would store this information on a excel worksheet on my computer which built up into quite a large set of data. I did miss a few days for various reasons, no racing through bad weather or personal reasons but, these were very few; about 10-20, no more..

. I had set the worksheet to calculate the individual bets as I went along both Win and E/W. For the each way I had a little program that automatically worked out the each way odds of each race i.e. ¼ or 1/5th the odds according to the type of race and runners. It involved 10 minutes work and a little copying and pasting each day. I devised some auto tables and formulas to calculate which bets were making a profit as I went along.

I started doing this on the 28th July 2011 and finished on the 27th July 2012.

NOTE: - Non Runners, I ignored non runners during this process. If a horse turned out to be a non runner then it was still included in the statistics and the bets. I could have checked for non runners each morning and adjusted my data but, I deemed it best not to. If I noted the first in the betting forecast was a non runner then I could have supplemented the second in the forecast in its place and so on. But, by the time the races started in the afternoon there were still likely to be non runners. So, all non runners were included in the statistics and bets. There were quite a few times in a lucky 15 for example that there were two winners and a non runner. How much this affected the bets I do not know but, I feel it may have been favourable to the bets in the long term. So, when and if you decide to utilise these statistics once you have read the book bear in mind the statistics were based on including non runners.

Horse Racing: the Statistical Route 2

THE BETS

10 different types of bets were studied against these statistics, 20 if including their E/W counterpart. They are as follows and include all six races unless indicated in brackets:-

- Win singles – E/W singles
- Win doubles – E/W doubles
- Win trebles – E/W trebles
- Win fourfolds – E/W fourfolds
- Win patent – E/W patent (first 3 races of the day only)
- Win lucky 15 – E/W lucky 15 (first 4 races of the day only)
- Win singles & doubles – E/W singles & doubles
- Win doubles&trebles – E/W doubles&trebles
- Win alpha bet – E/W alpha bet
- Win lucky 63 – E/W lucky 63

- Singles = 6 bets-a single bet on all 6 horses
- Doubles = 15 bets-15 permutations on all 6 horses.
- Trebles = 20 bets-20 permutations on all 6 horses
- Fourfolds = 15 bets-15 permutations on all 6 horses.
- Patent = 7 bets – 3 singles, 3 doubles, 1 treble for 3 horses
- Lucky 15 = 15 bets – 4 singles, 6 doubles, 4 trebles, 1 fourfold for 4 horses
- Singles & Doubles – 21 bets-21 permutations for 6 horses.
- Doubles & Trebles = 35 bets-35 permutations for 6 horses.
- Alpha Bet = 26 bets-6 singles, 12 doubles, 6 trebles, 1 fourfold, 1 sixfold for 6 horses (A special bet comprising of a patent first 3 horses, a patent last 3 horses, a yankee middle 4 horses and a sixfold all 6 horses)
- Lucky 63 = 63 bets-6 singles, 15 doubles, 20 trebles, 15 fourfolds, 6 fivefolds, 1 sixfold.

Multiply the above by 2 for their each way counterparts.

The next page is part one of the book but, do look at part 2 as I think this more pertinent. If you have any misunderstanding it will become clearer as you look at the tables further in the book.

Horse Racing: the Statistical Route 2

STATISTICS BY RACE TYPE

Below is the whole table by race type. I have sorted this into shorter categories further on but, I thought I ought to show the whole lot in one go at first.
The first column indicates the type of race and number of runners. These have been abbreviated and are as follows:-

hh	-	handicap hurdles
nh	-	non handicap hurdles
hch	-	handicap chases
nch	-	non handicap chases
haw	-	handicap all weather
naw	-	non handicap all weather
hf	-	handicap flat
nf	-	non handicap flat

These are further divided into four categories according to the number of runners i.e. 4-7, 8-11, 12-15 and 16+. So, in the first entry under "race type and number of runners hh4-7 = handicap hurdle of between 4 and 7 runners. (**Note**- claiming races and nursery races were judged as handicaps. Races with less than 4 runners were not included in these statistics).

The second column shows the amount of races of that type analysed. The third column shows the forecast bet position i.e. 1, 2, 3 and 4. The fourth column shows the win profit for that bet position to a £1 stake. The fifth column shows the E/W profit to a 50p E/W stake. The sixth column shows the percentage of winners for that forecast bet position and for that type of race. The seventh column shows same but for placed horses (win or placed).

Begins Next page:-

Horse Racing: the Statistical Route 2

TABLE 1: RACE TYPE - START

race type and num of runn	num of races anal	bet for pos	win pro	e/w pro	% win	% pla
hh4-7	27	1	-20	-14	11	44
hh8-11	67	1	2	-1	28	60
hh12-15	44	1	-16	-12	18	41
hh16+	25	1	0	1	24	48
nh4-7	84	1	33	16	65	77
nh8-11	166	1	24	7	45	70
nh12-15	120	1	-16	-8	33	71
nh16+	31	1	0	-1	39	71
hch4-7	73	1	-8	-16	26	44
hch8-11	58	1	-4	-12	21	41
hch12-15	17	1	2	0	29	53
hch16+	3	1	6	5	33	67
nch4-7	112	1	4	-6	50	67
nch8-11	16	1	2	-1	38	56
nch12-15	1	1	-1	-1	0	0
nch16+	1	1	-1	0	0	100
haw4-7	59	1	-1	-7	37	54
haw8-11	84	1	-9	-9	23	56
haw12-15	65	1	-24	-11	14	46
haw16+	1	1	-1	-1	0	0
naw4-7	61	1	0	-1	49	72
naw8-11	54	1	-1	-6	37	59
naw12-15	25	1	-9	-10	24	40
naw16+	0	1	0	0	na	na
hf4-7	46	1	-18	-16	22	43

CONTINUED NEXT PAGE

Horse Racing: the Statistical Route 2

TABLE 1: RACE TYPE - CONTINUED

race type and num of runn	num of races anal	bet for pos	win pro	e/w pro	% win	% pla
hf8-11	129	1	-21	-21	23	52
hf12-15	83	1	-23	-12	17	51
hf16+	65	1	-8	-1	14	43
nf4-7	116	1	-19	-18	37	60
nf8-11	164	1	-9	-12	35	65
nf12-15	110	1	-15	-10	28	65
nf16+	31	1	-10	-6	19	58
hh4-7	26	2	-1	0	31	62
hh8-11	69	2	-35	-22	10	48
hh12-15	46	2	-6	-10	15	30
hh16+	25	2	8	5	16	40
nh4-7	81	2	-23	-17	20	51
nh8-11	165	2	-10	-5	23	60
nh12-15	122	2	-5	-6	23	54
nh16+	30	2	0	0	27	57
hch4-7	76	2	-3	-8	24	43
hch8-11	58	2	6	0	22	50
hch12-15	15	2	-8	-5	7	40
hch16+	3	2	5	3	33	67
nch4-7	107	2	13	-4	33	50
nch8-11	16	2	11	5	25	56
nch12-15	1	2	3	2	100	100
nch16+	1	2	-1	-1	0	0
haw4-7	57	2	-20	-18	18	39
haw8-11	82	2	7	0	20	50

CONTINUED NEXT PAGE

Horse Racing: the Statistical Route 2

TABLE 1: RACE TYPE - CONTINUED

race type and num of runn	num of races anal	bet for pos	win pro	e/w pro	% win	% pla
haw12-15	60	2	-5	-3	12	40
haw16+	1	2	-1	-1	0	0
naw4-7	59	2	-10	-14	25	42
naw8-11	55	2	-21	-14	22	55
naw12-15	25	2	1	2	28	64
naw16+	0	2	0	0	na	na
hf4-7	44	2	-29	-27	9	23
hf8-11	131	2	-41	-29	15	49
hf12-15	87	2	-6	-9	15	38
hf16+	66	2	23	19	17	41
nf4-7	116	2	-1	-11	27	47
nf8-11	160	2	-32	-14	19	59
nf12-15	111	2	-47	-28	14	48
nf16+	29	2	1	0	17	48
hh4-7	27	3	2	-3	22	33
hh8-11	69	3	-36	-25	10	38
hh12-15	47	3	-14	-8	11	38
hh16+	23	3	-1	1	9	30
nh4-7	80	3	-28	-20	9	33
nh8-11	165	3	-47	-24	12	49
nh12-15	123	3	-7	2	12	48
nh16+	33	3	-11	-10	9	30
hch4-7	75	3	8	-5	21	37
hch8-11	56	3	21	7	20	41
hch12-15	17	3	4	0	24	35
hch16+	3	3	-3	-3	0	0

CONTINUED NEXT PAGE

Horse Racing: the Statistical Route 2

TABLE 1: RACE TYPE - CONTINUED

race type and num of runn	num of races anal	bet for pos	win pro	e/w pro	% win	% pla
nch4-7	109	3	-50	-46	13	28
nch8-11	17	3	-5	-6	12	24
nch12-15	1	3	-1	-1	0	0
nch16+	1	3	-1	-1	0	0
haw4-7	59	3	-19	-14	14	42
haw8-11	82	3	-4	-7	15	41
haw12-15	62	3	-40	-31	6	24
haw16+	0	3	0	0	na	na
naw4-7	60	3	9	8	22	48
naw8-11	51	3	-22	-19	12	35
naw12-15	25	3	-20	-15	4	32
naw16+	0	3	0	0	na	na
hf4-7	47	3	8	0	23	43
hf8-11	123	3	-10	-11	17	42
hf12-15	79	3	22	9	19	37
hf16+	68	3	-4	-13	9	24
nf4-7	116	3	0	-11	21	35
nf8-11	166	3	-63	-48	13	40
nf12-15	107	3	-18	-15	11	39
nf16+	30	3	3	-5	13	27
hh4-7	27	4	21	6	22	26
hh8-11	64	4	25	12	16	36
hh12-15	46	4	3	9	13	39
hh16+	23	4	5	6	9	43
nh4-7	77	4	-66	-58	3	10

CONTINUED NEXT PAGE

Horse Racing: the Statistical Route 2

TABLE 1: RACE TYPE - CONTINUED

race type and num of runn	num of races anal	bet for pos	win pro	e/w pro	% win	% pla
nh8-11	160	4	-41	-19	11	41
nh12-15	120	4	51	36	13	43
nh16+	31	4	-10	-3	10	35
hch4-7	76	4	-27	-27	12	26
hch8-11	57	4	-6	-2	12	44
hch12-15	16	4	-9	-6	6	25
hch16+	3	4	-3	-3	0	0
nch4-7	100	4	-45	-52	8	15
nch8-11	16	4	6	3	25	50
nch12-15	1	4	-1	0	0	100
nch16+	1	4	5	3	100	100
haw4-7	55	4	24	7	20	35
haw8-11	84	4	-12	-18	14	32
haw12-15	63	4	19	10	17	37
haw16+	1	4	-1	-1	0	0
naw4-7	61	4	-8	-14	10	23
naw8-11	54	4	-8	-7	15	35
naw12-15	24	4	-1	2	8	38
naw16+	0	4	0	0	na	na
hf4-7	46	4	54	27	33	43
hf8-11	120	4	-44	-41	9	28
hf12-15	81	4	-39	-30	6	26
hf16+	67	4	-26	-27	6	18
nf4-7	113	4	-4	-12	11	29
nf8-11	160	4	10	-8	14	35
nf12-15	110	4	-20	-26	11	29
nf16+	27	4	1	-3	7	26

TABLE 1: RACE TYPE - END

Horse Racing: the Statistical Route 2

WIN PROFIT

IMPORTANT NOTE - The following tables have had entries removed where less than 20 races were analysed from table 1.

The table below gives the statistics sorted into win profit only from table 1, giving the highest first. The win profit column shows the results rounded to the nearest £1

TABLE 2: WIN PROFIT – START

race type and num of runners	num of races analyzed	bet forecast pos	win profit £
hf4-7	46	4	54
nh12-15	120	4	51
nh4-7	84	1	33
hh8-11	64	4	25
nh8-11	166	1	24
haw4-7	55	4	24
hf16+	66	2	23
hf12-15	79	3	22
hh4-7	27	4	21
hch8-11	56	3	21
haw12-15	63	4	19
nch4-7	107	2	13
nf8-11	160	4	10
naw4-7	60	3	9
hch4-7	75	3	8
hh16+	25	2	8
hf4-7	47	3	8
haw8-11	82	2	7
hch8-11	58	2	6

CONTINUED NEXT PAGE

Horse Racing: the Statistical Route 2

TABLE 2: WIN PROFIT – CONTINUED

race type and num of runners	num of races analyzed	bet forecast pos	win profit £
hh16+	23	4	5
nch4-7	112	1	4
nf16+	30	3	3
hh12-15	46	4	3
hh4-7	27	3	2
hh8-11	67	1	2
naw12-15	25	2	1
nf16+	27	4	1
nf16+	29	2	1
naw4-7	61	1	0
hh16+	25	1	0
nf4-7	116	3	0
nh16+	30	2	0
nh16+	31	1	0
naw12-15	24	4	-1
nf4-7	116	2	-1
hh16+	23	3	-1
hh4-7	26	2	-1
haw4-7	59	1	-1
naw8-11	54	1	-1
hch4-7	76	2	-3
nf4-7	113	4	-4
haw8-11	82	3	-4
hf16+	68	3	-4
hch8-11	58	1	-4
haw12-15	60	2	-5

CONTINUED NEXT PAGE

Horse Racing: the Statistical Route 2

TABLE 2: WIN PROFIT – CONTINUED

race type and num of runners	num of races analyzed	bet forecast pos	win profit £
nh12-15	122	2	-5
hch8-11	57	4	-6
hh12-15	46	2	-6
hf12-15	87	2	-6
nh12-15	123	3	-7
hf16+	65	1	-8
naw4-7	61	4	-8
naw8-11	54	4	-8
hch4-7	73	1	-8
haw8-11	84	1	-9
nf8-11	164	1	-9
naw12-15	25	1	-9
nh8-11	165	2	-10
hf8-11	123	3	-10
nf16+	31	1	-10
nh16+	31	4	-10
naw4-7	59	2	-10
nh16+	33	3	-11
haw8-11	84	4	-12
hh12-15	47	3	-14
nf12-15	110	1	-15
nh12-15	120	1	-16
hh12-15	44	1	-16
nf12-15	107	3	-18
hf4-7	46	1	-18

CONTINUED NEXT PAGE

Horse Racing: the Statistical Route 2

TABLE 2: WIN PROFIT – CONTINUED

race type and num of runners	num of races analyzed	bet forecast pos	win profit £
nf4-7	116	1	-19
haw4-7	59	3	-19
nf12-15	110	4	-20
hh4-7	27	1	-20
naw12-15	25	3	-20
haw4-7	57	2	-20
hf8-11	129	1	-21
naw8-11	55	2	-21
naw8-11	51	3	-22
nh4-7	81	2	-23
hf12-15	83	1	-23
haw12-15	65	1	-24
hf16+	67	4	-26
hch4-7	76	4	-27
nh4-7	80	3	-28
ht4-7	44	2	-29
nf8-11	160	2	-32
hh8-11	69	2	-35
hh8-11	69	3	-36
hf12-15	81	4	-39
haw12-15	62	3	-40
hf8-11	131	2	-41
nh8-11	160	4	-41
hf8-11	120	4	-44
nch4-7	100	4	-45

CONTINUED NEXT PAGE

Horse Racing: the Statistical Route 2

TABLE 2: WIN PROFIT – CONTINUED

race type and num of runners	num of races analyzed	bet forecast pos	win profit £
nf12-15	111	2	-47
nch4-7	109	3	-50
nf8-11	166	3	-63
nh4-7	77	4	-66

TABLE 2: WIN PROFIT – END

Horse Racing: the Statistical Route 2

PLACE (E/W) PROFIT

The table below gives the statistics sorted into E/W profit only from table 1, giving the highest first (50p e/w-50p win and 50p place). The E/W profit column shows the results rounded to the nearest £1

TABLE 3: PLACE (E/W) PROFIT - START

race type and num of runn	num of races anal	bet for pos	e/w pro £
nh12-15	120	4	36
hf4-7	46	4	27
hf16+	66	2	19
nh4-7	84	1	16
hh8-11	64	4	12
haw12-15	63	4	10
hh12-15	46	4	9
hf12-15	79	3	9
naw4-7	60	3	8
nh0-11	100	1	7
haw4-7	55	4	7
hch8-11	56	3	7
hh4-7	27	4	6
hh16+	23	4	6
hh16+	25	2	5
nh12-15	123	3	2
naw12-15	24	4	2
naw12-15	25	2	2
hh16+	25	1	1
hh16+	23	3	1
hch8-11	58	2	0

CONTINUED NEXT PAGE

Horse Racing: the Statistical Route 2

TABLE 3: PLACE (E/W) PROFIT - CONTINUED

race type and num of runners	num of races analyzed	bet forecast pos	e/w pro £
nf16+	29	2	0
hh4-7	26	2	0
hf4-7	47	3	0
haw8-11	82	2	0
nh16+	30	2	0
hh8-11	67	1	-1
nh16+	31	1	-1
naw4-7	61	1	-1
hf16+	65	1	-1
hch8-11	57	4	-2
nh16+	31	4	-3
hh4-7	27	3	-3
nf16+	27	4	-3
haw12-15	60	2	-3
nch4-7	107	2	-4
hch4-7	75	3	-5
nf16+	30	3	-5
nh8-11	165	2	-5
nch4-7	112	1	-6
naw8-11	54	1	-6
nf16+	31	1	-6
nh12-15	122	2	-6
haw8-11	82	3	-7
naw8-11	54	4	-7
haw4-7	59	1	-7

CONTINUED NEXT PAGE

Horse Racing: the Statistical Route 2

TABLE 3: PLACE (E/W) PROFIT - CONTINUED

race type and num of runners	num of races analyzed	bet forecast pos	e/w pro £
hh12-15	47	3	-8
nf8-11	160	4	-8
nh12-15	120	1	-8
hch4-7	76	2	-8
haw8-11	84	1	-9
hf12-15	87	2	-9
naw12-15	25	1	-10
hh12-15	46	2	-10
nh16+	33	3	-10
nf12-15	110	1	-10
nf4-7	116	2	-11
hf8-11	123	3	-11
haw12-15	65	1	-11
nf4-7	116	3	-11
hch8-11	58	1	-12
nf4-7	113	4	-12
hf12-15	83	1	-12
hh12-15	44	1	-12
nf8-11	164	1	-12
hf16+	68	3	-13
nf8-11	160	2	-14
naw4-7	59	2	-14
naw4-7	61	4	-14
haw4-7	59	3	-14
naw8-11	55	2	-14

CONTINUED NEXT PAGE

Horse Racing: the Statistical Route 2

TABLE 3: PLACE (E/W) PROFIT – CONTINUED

race type and num of runners	num of races analyzed	bet forecast pos	e/w pro £
hf8-11	120	4	-41
nch4-7	109	3	-46
nf8-11	166	3	-48
nch4-7	100	4	-52
nh4-7	77	4	-58

TABLE 3: PLACE (E/W) PROFIT END

Horse Racing: the Statistical Route 2

WIN PERCENTAGE

The table below gives the statistics sorted into a percentage of how often a horse in the betting forecast wins against the number of races analysed regardless of profit. For example:- the first column shows that the 1st horse in the betting forecast for novice hurdles of between 4 and 11 runners has won 65% of those races.

TABLE 4: WIN PERCENTAGE: START

race type and num of runners	num of races analyzed	bet forecast pos	win %
nh4-7	84	1	65
nch4-7	112	1	50
naw4-7	61	1	49
nh8-11	166	1	45
nh16+	31	1	39
haw4-7	59	1	37
naw8-11	54	1	37
nf4-7	116	1	37
nf8-11	164	1	35
hf4-7	46	4	33
nch4-7	107	2	33
nh12-15	120	1	33
hh4-7	26	2	31
hh8-11	67	1	28
naw12-15	25	2	28
nf12-15	110	1	28
nh16+	30	2	27
nf4-7	116	2	27
hch4-7	73	1	26
naw4-7	59	2	25

CONTINUED NEXT PAGE

Horse Racing: the Statistical Route 2

TABLE 4: WIN PERCENTAGE: CONTINUED

race type and num of runners	num of races analyzed	bet forecast pos	win %
hh16+	25	1	24
hch4-7	76	2	24
naw12-15	25	1	24
hf4-7	47	3	23
nh12-15	122	2	23
haw8-11	84	1	23
nh8-11	165	2	23
hf8-11	129	1	23
hh4-7	27	4	22
naw4-7	60	3	22
hch8-11	58	2	22
hh4-7	27	3	22
hf4-7	46	1	22
naw8-11	55	2	22
hch4-7	75	3	21
nf4-7	116	3	21
hch8-11	58	1	21
haw4-7	55	4	20
hch8-11	56	3	20
haw8-11	82	2	20
nh4-7	81	2	20
hf12-15	79	3	19
nf16+	31	1	19
nf8-11	160	2	19
hh12-15	44	1	18

CONTINUED NEXT PAGE

Horse Racing: the Statistical Route 2

TABLE 4: WIN PERCENTAGE: CONTINUED

race type and num of runners	num of races analyzed	bet forecast pos	win %
haw4-7	57	2	18
hf16+	66	2	17
haw12-15	63	4	17
nf16+	29	2	17
hf8-11	123	3	17
hf12-15	83	1	17
hh8-11	64	4	16
hh16+	25	2	16
haw8-11	82	3	15
hh12-15	46	2	15
hf12-15	87	2	15
naw8-11	54	4	15
hf8-11	131	2	15
nf8-11	160	4	14
hf16+	65	1	14
haw8-11	84	4	14
haw4-7	59	3	14
haw12-15	65	1	14
nf12-15	111	2	14
nh12-15	120	4	13
nf16+	30	3	13
hh12-15	46	4	13
nch4-7	109	3	13
nf8-11	166	3	13
haw12-15	60	2	12

CONTINUED NEXT PAGE

Horse Racing: the Statistical Route 2

TABLE 4: WIN PERCENTAGE: CONTINUED

race type and num of runners	num of races analyzed	bet forecast pos	win %
hch8-11	57	4	12
nh12-15	123	3	12
naw8-11	51	3	12
hch4-7	76	4	12
nh8-11	165	3	12
nf4-7	113	4	11
hh12-15	47	3	11
nf12-15	107	3	11
nf12-15	110	4	11
hh4-7	27	1	11
nh8-11	160	4	11
naw4-7	61	4	10
nh16+	31	4	10
hh8-11	69	2	10
hh8-11	69	3	10
hh16+	23	4	9
hh16+	23	3	9
hf16+	68	3	9
nh16+	33	3	9
nh4-7	80	3	9
hf4-7	44	2	9
hf8-11	120	4	9
naw12-15	24	4	8
nch4-7	100	4	8
nf16+	27	4	7

CONTINUED NEXT PAGE

Horse Racing: the Statistical Route 2

TABLE 4: WIN PERCENTAGE: CONTINUED

race type and num of runners	num of races analyzed	bet forecast pos	win %
hf16+	67	4	6
hf12-15	81	4	6
haw12-15	62	3	6
naw12-15	25	3	4
nh4-7	77	4	3

TABLE 4: WIN PERCENTAGE: END

Horse Racing: the Statistical Route 2

PLACE PERCENTAGE

The table below gives the statistics sorted into percentage PLACED (win and placed) obtain against the number of races analysed for each type of race.

TABLE 5: PLACE (E/W) PERCENTAGE - START

race type and num of runners	num of races analyzed	bet forecast pos	place e/w %
nh4-7	84	1	77
naw4-7	61	1	72
nh16+	31	1	71
nh12-15	120	1	71
nh8-11	166	1	70
nch4-7	112	1	67
nf8-11	164	1	65
nf12-15	110	1	65
naw12-15	25	2	64
hh4-7	26	2	62
hh8-11	67	1	60
nh8-11	165	2	60
nf4-7	116	1	60
naw8-11	54	1	59
nf8-11	160	2	59
nf16+	31	1	58
nh16+	30	2	57
haw8-11	84	1	56
naw8-11	55	2	55
haw4-7	59	1	54
nh12-15	122	2	54

CONTINUED NEXT PAGE

Horse Racing: the Statistical Route 2

TABLE 5: PLACE (E/W) PERCENTAGE – CONTINUED

race type and num of runners	num of races analyzed	bet forecast pos	place e/w %
hf8-11	129	1	52
nh4-7	81	2	51
hf12-15	83	1	51
nch4-7	107	2	50
haw8-11	82	2	50
hch8-11	58	2	50
hf8-11	131	2	49
nh8-11	165	3	49
naw4-7	60	3	48
nf16+	29	2	48
hh16+	25	1	48
nh12-15	123	3	48
hh8-11	69	2	48
nf12-15	111	2	48
nf4-7	116	2	47
haw12-15	65	1	46
hch8-11	57	4	44
hch4-7	73	1	44
hh4-7	27	1	44
hf4-7	46	4	43
nh12-15	120	4	43
hf4-7	47	3	43
hh16+	23	4	43
hch4-7	76	2	43

CONTINUED NEXT PAGE

Horse Racing: the Statistical Route 2

TABLE 5: PLACE (E/W) PERCENTAGE – CONTINUED

race type and num of runners	num of races analyzed	bet forecast pos	place e/w %
hf16+	65	1	43
hf4-7	46	1	43
hf8-11	123	3	42
naw4-7	59	2	42
haw4-7	59	3	42
hf16+	66	2	41
hch8-11	56	3	41
haw8-11	82	3	41
hch8-11	58	1	41
hh12-15	44	1	41
nh8-11	160	4	41
hh16+	25	2	40
haw12-15	60	2	40
naw12-15	25	1	40
nf8-11	166	3	40
hh12-15	46	4	39
nf12-15	107	3	39
haw4-7	57	2	39
naw12-15	24	4	38
hf12-15	87	2	38
hh12-15	47	3	38
hh8-11	69	3	38
hf12-15	79	3	37
haw12-15	63	4	37
hch4-7	75	3	37

CONTINUED NEXT PAGE

Horse Racing: the Statistical Route 2

TABLE 5: PLACE (E/W) PERCENTAGE – CONTINUED

race type and num of runners	num of races analyzed	bet forecast pos	place e/w %
hh8-11	64	4	36
haw4-7	55	4	35
nf8-11	160	4	35
nf4-7	116	3	35
naw8-11	54	4	35
nh16+	31	4	35
naw8-11	51	3	35
hh4-7	27	3	33
nh4-7	80	3	33
haw8-11	84	4	32
naw12-15	25	3	32
hh16+	23	3	30
hh12-15	46	2	30
nh16+	33	3	30
nf4-7	113	4	29
nf12-15	110	4	29
hf8-11	120	4	28
nch4-7	109	3	28
nf16+	30	3	27
hh4-7	27	4	26
nf16+	27	4	26
hch4-7	76	4	26
hf12-15	81	4	26
hf16+	68	3	24
haw12-15	62	3	24

CONTINUED NEXT PAGE

Horse Racing: the Statistical Route 2

TABLE 5: PLACE (E/W) PERCENTAGE – CONTINUED

race type and num of runners	num of races analyzed	bet forecast pos	place e/w %
naw4-7	61	4	23
hf4-7	44	2	23
hf16+	67	4	18
nch4-7	100	4	15
nh4-7	77	4	10

TABLE 5: PLACE (E/W) PERCENTAGE – END

SOME NOTES AND THOUGHTS

I did not make much headway with these statistics. About half way through the year I thought I would try and utilise these statistics into something useful and profitable by applying them to the whole of the race card each day. I tried finding the best statistics from the whole race card; not just the first 6 races. I utilised all of the above tables in some way, cherry picking the most win profitable, the best place profitable, the best percentage win ratios and place ratios. For example-I would look for races of handicap flat with 4-7 runners and bet on the 4th forecast horse as these showed the most profit. I would then look for any nh12-15 runner race; the second most profitable and work down the table until I had 4 or 6 horses and put them into a lucky 15 or a lucky 63. I tried the same for the table showing the most percentage win rate and E/W types of bets as well.

    I conducted several experiments with different types of bets but, the problem was, I just could not seem to make a profit out it. I did not, in truth, do it for long enough to make a fair assessment but, I just was not encouraged by early results. Theoretically it should work and the chances of getting a few winners or placed horses in a multi bet should be high; it just did not work out that way. However, I should have conducted these experiments for a longer period as I only did so for 4-6 weeks at a time. At the time the tables looked a bit different from how they are now, the maximum profits showing at the time were around £30 and some of the race types at the top of the table were different. So, whether it could work better now, having completed the whole year, I do not know. So, I leave it for you to make something of them and I only publish them as they provide some interesting statistics. You may want to utilise them in into some kind of strategy of your own and they may prove useful in that respect, but I would be cautious. For me, the next part of this book shows some more positive results and is far simpler to follow.

Horse Racing: the Statistical Route 2

PROFIT/LOSS BY BET TYPE

Below is the whole profit/loss table (divided into 2 parts) showing all the results. The first column shows Win or E/W. The second column shows the forecast betting number i.e. first in the betting, second in the betting and so on. The following 10 columns show the type of bet applied to those 1st, 2nd, 3rd and 4th in the betting forecasts win and E/W. Only the first 6 races of any given day have been analysed and only the 1st, 2nd, 3rd or 4th horses in the Racing Post betting forecast have been used. (I have had to split the table in two for use of space).

	Forecast position	singles	doubles	trebles	fours	patent
win	1st	-82.86	-148.44	-167.78	-143.84	-124.93
win	2nd	-113.74	-206.49	-226.3	-460.34	-154.76
win	3rd	-162.2	-336.1	-448.31	-620.38	-7.35
win	4th	-72.67	-176.65	-355.14	-502.4	73.22
e/w	1st	-91.97	-168.57	-217.05	-244.73	-124.54
e/w	2nd	-105.11	-190.42	-235.07	-389.46	-168.22
e/w	3rd	-158.09	-288.74	-355.87	-403.69	-84.19
e/w	4th	-116.89	-222.54	-350.83	-479.68	-102.22

	Forecast position	lucky 15	sin+dou	dou+tre	lucky 63	alpha
win	1st	-9.64	-111.33	-159.39	-159.42	-194.66
win	2nd	258.45	-179.99	-217.81	-331.72	-238.32
win	3rd	-283.67	-286.41	-400.22	-496.41	-376.81
win	4th	641.31	-146.94	-278.65	-394.34	-153.48
e/w	1st	-93.3	-146.68	-196.27	-216.06	-199.23
e/w	2nd	36.75	-166.04	-215.93	-292.51	-202.91
e/w	3rd	-228.75	-251.41	-327.1	-338.65	-287.73
e/w	4th	164.47	-192.35	-295.85	-384.38	-237.37

Horse Racing: the Statistical Route 2

In each bet type a £3 total stake was analysed- as follows:-

Singles = 6 bets @ 50p win or 12 bets @ 25p e/w. Total £3
Doubles = 15 bets @ 20p win or 30 bets @ 10p e/w. Total £3
Trebles = 20 bets @ 15p win or 40 bets @ 7.5p e/w. Total £3
Fourfolds = 15 bets @ 20p win or 30 bets@10p e/w. Total £3
Patent = 7 bets @ 43p win or 14 bets @ 21p e/w. Total £3
Lucky 15 = 15 bets @ 20p win or 30 bets @ 10p e/w. Total £3
Singles & Doubles = 21 bets @ 14p win or 42 bets @ 07p e/w. Total £3
Doubles & Trebles = 35 bets @ 09p win or 70 bets @ 04p e/w. Total £3
Lucky 63 = 63 bets @ 5p win or 126 bets @ 2p e/w. Total £3
Alpha Bet = 26 bets @ 12p win or 52 bets @ 6p e/w. Total £3

Please note the above has been rounded to the nearest whole number. The actual results were calculated to 5 decimal places. For example-in the case of the Lucky 63 win it equals £3 dived by 63 bets which = 0.047619 pence. Of course in practice this amount would not be acceptable as a bet in a book maker.
You can proportion the amount of profit up or down accordingly. For example 0.047619 pence would read better as .05 pence and the profit would show as slightly higher or lower.

The next table shows the same table from page 31 but, with only the profitable results showing.

		Forecast position	patent	lucky 15
win	1st			
win	2nd			258.45
win	3rd			
win	4th		73.22	641.31
e/w	1st			
e/w	2nd			36.75
e/w	3rd			
e/w	4th			164.47

In the UK most bookmakers offer a bonus for lucky 15's and lucky 63's. If there is only one winner they will give 3 times the odds on a lucky 15 and 5 times the odds for a lucky 63. This only applies to the win part of the bet and providing there are no non runners occurring in the bet. I calculated the bonuses that applied over the whole year for those bets and the next table shows what these bonuses would have been for lucky 15's and lucky 63's:-

Horse Racing: the Statistical Route 2

	Forecast position	bonus lucky 15	bonus lucky 63
win	1st	19.98	3.62
win	2nd	45.65	7.66
win	3rd	85.86	24.94
win	4th	153.89	55.11
e/w	1st	9.99	1.81
e/w	2nd	22.825	3.83
e/w	3rd	42.93	12.47
e/w	4th	76.945	27.555

By adding those bonuses to the profit table it would look like this; only the profitable results are shown:-

	Forecast position	patent	lucky 15
win	1st		10.34
win	2nd		304.1
win	3rd		
win	4th	73.22	795.2
e/w	1st		
e/w	2nd		59.58
e/w	3rd		
e/w	4th		241.4

Let me sum that up for you; if you had gone into a book maker and had a 20p win lucky 15 on the second in the betting forecast for the first four races every day you would have made a profit of £304.10 over the year period with bonuses. A 20p win lucky 15 applied to the fourth in the betting forecast for the same races would have netted £795.20 profit with bonuses.

I would like to just apply one more set of statistics to the above table. I recorded through the year just how many times a return of over £3 occurred for the above bets and how many times a return of more than zero occurred for the above bets. The following table shows how that turned out percentage wise:-

Horse Racing: the Statistical Route 2

BET	OVER £3 OCCURANCE	OVER £0 OCCURANCE
lucky 15 win 2nd bet	14%	63%
patent win 4th bet	19%	42%
lucky 15 win 4th bet	12%	54%
lucky 15 each way 2nd bet	22%	93%
lucky 15 each way 4th bet	16%	86%

I felt this was worth showing. Any betting statistics are going to have losing runs and this can be very dispiriting. What this table shows is that although for example doing an each way lucky 15 on the fourth bet would be less profitable than doing it win. It does show that you will more often get some profit or, at least some money back each day. I just felt it was worth showing this as it may affect your judgement; it is a matter for personal preference.

A NOTE ABOUT NON RUNNERS

I have already mentioned this but, the statistics include non runners. The first four in the betting forecasts include these. I did not note a non runner and then select the next horse in the forecast. In some cases if I had done this I would have been selecting the 5th or even the 6th and 7th in the forecasts on occasions; it was always the first 4 whatever the situation. I feel that in most cases this is an advantage; you can have two good winners in a lucky 15 and a non runner and still get a decent return which might not be the case if the horse had ran and lost although I appreciate it could have won. Also, you can only have one winner of a race but, you can have a winner on one bet and a non runner on another if you are trying two types of bet in the same races. There are times when there are lots of non runners due to bad weather for example and a bet might end up a bit pointless. You could end up with 3 non runners on a 4 horse bet but, it does not happen often in practice and you do not lose the bet. And ironing out the non runners and doing 5th and 6th's in the forecasts would have complicated things a lot. As always it is your choice but, bear in mind the statistics have been compiled in this way; always the first four in the betting forecasts; non runners or not.

Horse Racing: the Statistical Route 2

MY SUMMARY

There were some surprises along the way; I thought some of the lesser bets like singles and doubles would show to be more profitable than the multi type bets. For professional gamblers this is probably the case but, they do have a different approach to gambling than anything tried in this book. I think the statistics show that trying bets with more than 4 selections is pushing it too far taking into account the reduced stake money. In fact at no time during the year did 6 winners occur in one day. Of course it may happen one day but, personally I would not bet my money based on the slim chance it will. All the profitable bets have turned out on the 4 horse selection bets i.e. lucky 15's in the first four races of the day, except for one exception; the patent for the fourth bet.

There is some logic to the results; it comes down to the ratio between frequency of win and the odds. The frequency of winners and placed horses decreases from 1ST, 2nd, 3rd and 4th forecasts but, the odds increase. The odds increase enough to make the 2nd and 4th forecasts profitable. This does leave a question mark over why the 3rd forecasts bets did not show a similar profit in relation to the other two. I do not have a very good answer to that but, I think it could have something to do with the way the public bet on horses. A lot of gambling concentrates on 3 horses in races and a third horse can become a shorter price than it's worth. So the ratio between win frequency and odds can be not as good for the 3rd forecasts than for the 2nd and 4th. The ratio for the 1st does not appear to be very good; a high frequency win rate but the odds are too low.

For me personally, I am happy with the result overall. It could have all been negative results and a waste of time on my part. However, I am satisfied that it has shown something that would be easy to do, very little work involved and the possibilities of profits, which was I set out to do.

A WORD OF WARNING

Of course the big question is – will the same bets produce a profit every year? I really do not know and I cannot guarantee they will; it is still a gamble. In truth it would be desirable to see it happen over a 10 or a 20 year period but, I have what I have and can only submit that. I have given my opinions in the preceding paragraphs but, they are only my opinions, not facts. It is important to me that you make your own mind up as to how, and what way, if at all, you are going to encompass the statistics of this book into your own arrangements. It is not my responsibility; it is your money and your decision. Sorry if that is a bit too succinct but, it has to be said and I am sure you understand that. My job has been to show the statistics, without any bias, with honesty and as clearly as possible.

The statistics are honest and given without any slant or manipulation on my part but, my opinions are a different matter; they are only a personal view. I give those opinions because I have had a longer time to think about the statistics than you and think those opinions will help you but, at the end of the day, you have to formulate your own judgement but, please be careful. It is always my fear that someone will be rash and go and spend all their life savings and lose it over a few weeks because of something I have said. Make sure you understand all the statistics given and that my opinion, where given, is just that, an opinion.

Horse Racing: the Statistical Route 2

The statistics are a long term study but, I also appreciate they are not based on anything real. Someone has compiled a betting forecast and for one year some of the aspects of those forecasts have proven to be profitable. It fulfilled my remit of trying to find something easy to do; did not require lots of typing each day, required collecting lots of statistics about form lines, types of going, jockeys, weights etc. Something simple that anyone could understand.

My first book "Horse Racing the Statistical Route" did require this and was very time consuming and a bit complicated. It was not designed to be a book and I published it because I felt it could provide some useful information. I have considered incorporating the work from that into these statistics but, then it would just complicate things and go against my remit for something simple and easy. I also thought I could have done more with these statistics and included other information as I went along but, again the same reasons prevented me from doing this, keep it very simple.

I have started to continue keeping the same statistics so, there might be a third book, I will see where I am in a years time. I don't think I can be as religious in keeping the records for another whole year. I have been doing this on and off for about 8/10 years and I am a bit out of fresh ideas for horse racing. Anyway that's for the future. In the meantime just heed my warnings and take them into account before you make any decisions about where and how you use your money.

    Thank You.
    GOOD LUCK. Mark Gaster

Horse Racing: the Statistical Route 2

ALSO BY THE AUTHOR

"HORSE RACING the STATISTICAL ROUTE" (part 1)

This book provides a valuable insight into which horses win and just as importantly, which ones lose. In all, 1374 races have been analysed by computer in a unique way, not by the <u>actual</u> best last place form or best average form but, best last place form and best average form in relation to other horses in the race. Also full analysis on days since last run, course winners, distance winners, top trainers, weight, top jockey and ratings. Plus, 566 of the 1374 races have been analysed to show profit and loss margins. The information is displayed in easy to follow tables and should not only be of interest to gamblers but, bookmakers, trainers, jockeys owners etc; in fact anybody with an interest in horse racing. The races have been divided into race types such as handicap hurdles, non handicap hurdles, handicap all weather etc. These groups have further been subdivided into 2 groups of runners i.e. 4-11 runners or 12+ runners, 16 groups in all. As a means of reading and really understanding the form of race horses this book will be invaluable.

"THE FRESHWATER FISHING CONDITIONS BOOK"

A statistical analysis of the conditions of month, wind speed, wind direction, weather, air temperatures, water temperatures, barometric pressure, water colour and moon phase in relation to coarse fishing. For tench, carp, bream, roach, chub, big/roach, crucian carp and rudd.

BOOKS LISTED online at:-

LULU PRESS-LULU.COM

And generally

Horse Racing: the Statistical Route 2

INDEX

A NOTE ABOUT NON RUNNERS	-	34
ABOUT STATISTICS	-	3
ABOUT THE BOOK	-	2
ALSO BY THE AUTHOR	-	37
HOW THE INFORMATION WAS COLLECTED	-	4
MY SUMMARY	-	35
PLACE (E/W) PROFIT	-	17
PLACE PERCENTAGE	-	26
PROFIT/LOSS BY BET TYPE	-	31
SOME NOTES AND THOUGHTS	-	30
STATISTICS BY RACE TYPE	-	6
TABLE 1: RACE TYPE - START	-	7
TABLE 2: WIN PROFIT - START	-	12
TABLE 3: PLACE (E/W) PROFIT - START	-	17
TABLE 4: WIN PERCENTAGE: START	-	21
TABLE 5: PLACE (E/W) PERCENTAGE - START	-	26
THE BETS	-	5
WIN PERCENTAGE	-	21
WIN PROFIT	-	12

Printed in Dunstable, United Kingdom